EMPTY

In the depths of the bowel.

A collection of thoughts...

Suffocating under the thick weight of the dark skies all my
filthy memories are reappearing. It is the Eve of Mankind
and I am nowhere now. I am in nothing. I believe that I
am in hell therefore I am. I am here. I am still here.
Waiting...

The wolf, gnashing her teeth and hissing flames, howls under the thicket and shadow of the midnight sky; spitting out the trembling remains of the wormeaten poor and the ravages of heaven, like her, I consume myself.

As I weep it rains softly on the town, the moonlight
sprinkles tears on the petals of the forest leaves while
crystaline dew drops trickel down the stems, and thunder
screams inside me under a dark blue winter's sky.

The rotten fruit of childhood lingers in the air while melancholy chokes the nape; tormented ever so long in perpetual unrest waiting to arrive at the point of the unknown by disordering all the senses but the stench of nauseating memories have hauntingly shaped my debauched existence.

Over bays of dead love, rolling on open wounds through
the misty air and the tiring sea; in anguish through the still
and torturous waters and air; in the grip of torment and pain
which laughs at me; in their hideously tumultuous silence;
just to get to you; my one true love.

I am a hanged man who wears his necktie of shame on the guillotine while silently under the pillars of blue, past comets tails, and the inter winding of the universe; there is an enormous stirring without chaos. It roams through the luminous heavens and from it's flaming bow lets fall shooting stars.

The youth, provoked and filled with this deep unhealing
wound faces the ugliness of this world; shudders, and with
his back to the dark wall and his heart full of dispair
storms at the universe.

In the fetal position weeping like a heavy baby without
eyes, I cry puddles of blood at the foot of my bed.

I see death toll the bitter taste of ashes that float on the air-
the stifling smell of wood suffocating on the black coal
smoked fire - drowned lilies - havoc on the avenues - and
than the misty haze of corpses covering the cemetery
fields.

The mother, hands sore from slapping, leaves satisfied
without seeing the piercing stares or the icy eyes under the
forehead full of welts; the door slams, the soul of her child
has given over to loathing. In the room, he relishes in the
dark desiring to achieve disorder and pity while unfolding
the puzzled sky. Later that night with the plan underway,
he lies on a soaked red bed, wrist slit, blood drips and seeps
through the cracks on the floor. The poor soul can finally
rest and dream of meadows full of love and not beatings
where waves of light vertigo high collapse and retire calmly
stir and take flight.

What does it matter to this dark stranger, the heart; the sheets of blood, of fire, and a thousand other murders, with a long sobbing howl of rage trailing from the inferno destroying every kind of joy in its wake.

Trembling, I watch the earth melt around me and the North Winds blow across this wreckage with only bitter pain and misery accompanying me. It nest in the pit of my being chilling me even more with vengeance for the past loves in my life. Killing my conscience. Nothing is here in my soul but it is still desired more. Look at how she weeps under the moon and stars at home. Her breath, in hand, is all there is for company. Her sheets are icy waters without reflections, and without a spring, gray; a boat in motionless waters. She is paying for the others while her abandoned cold room screams out for my sinister corruptions in the heart of her hallowed bed to be avenged.

But like a thousand dark angels, I part on the roadway, quite and sinister race, fleeing from my crime . She alone and afraid screams out for me to come back.

The stars have wept in the heart of her ears. The
infinitesimal land rolled white from her nape to the small
of her back; the sea has broken at her nipples; and I bleed
black at her royal side.

Black robe, black cape flowing in the breeze under the
black flag that beats above the black canopy on the gray
bricked gothic street a red rose glimmers through the
deluge.

The room is full of shadows you can hear the sad soft
whimpering which shudders and rises. The mist chills
trailing the folds of it snowy garment while smiling at me
through the teared up window and then shivers. I become
icy.

Refuge from my own mind, from the dread that I harbor,
hijacked dreams choke on mementos from the past, a mouthful
of lost thoughts.

Complacency eats at my rotting soul while I bleed demons and
my passion falls.

It melts through like butter against my skin. The shimmering blade, dulled by the penetrating of the flesh, weeps a little blood into the pool on the floor.

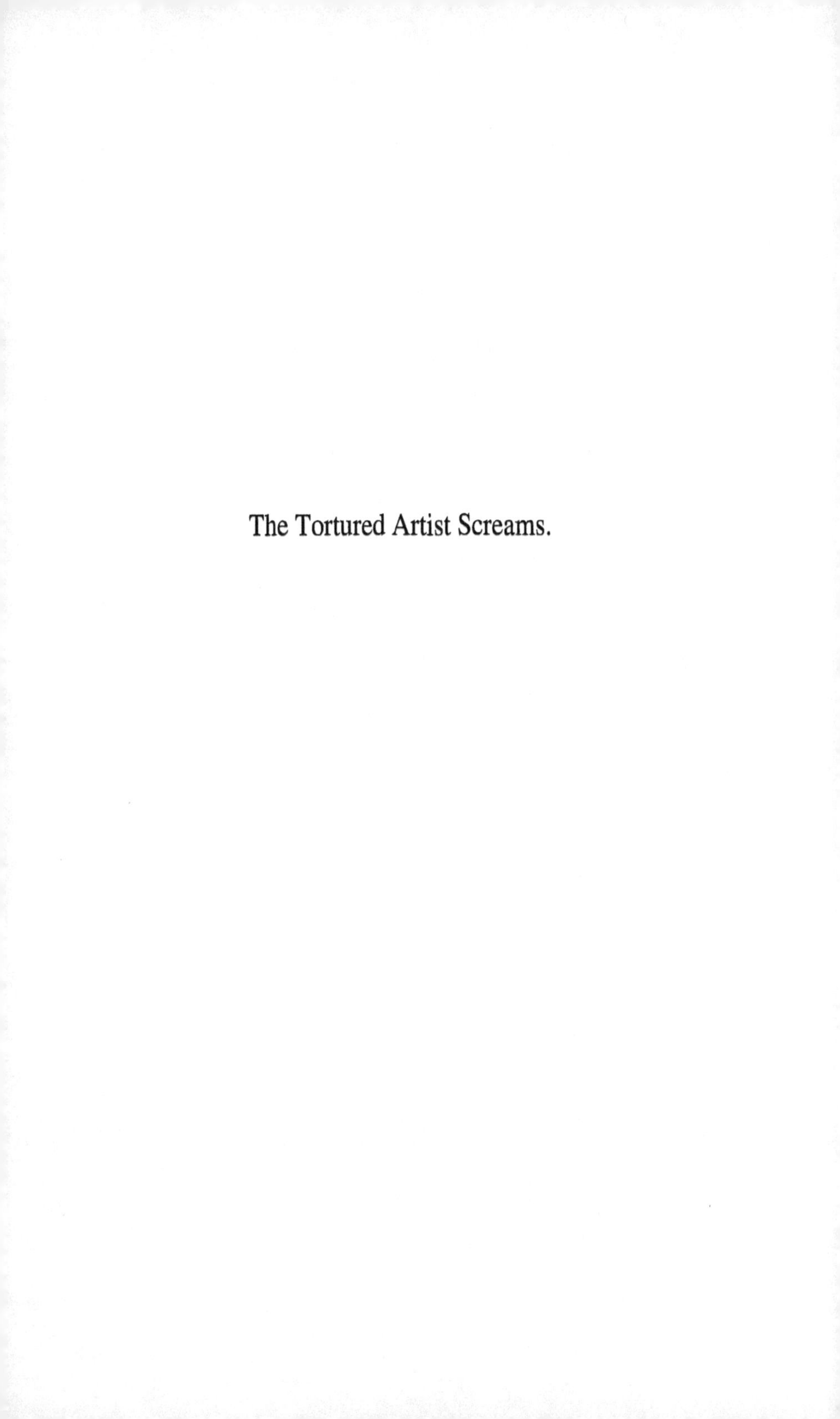

The Tortured Artist Screams.

My grey eyes cry and I sink deeper into the winter of my
being. The secrets held in a guilty heart stare back at me.
A condemned life lead in a cold storage of self rage pierces
through me. My grey eyes continue to cry. The flowers
say goodbye to the dead girl buried in my mind. I listen,
trembling, to the hollow echo hitting.
Everything is bitter to me today. I am made of glass.
Nothing can make the memory fade or can replace for me
the bleeding heart scarred by the departure and onslaught
of rain on a cold dark cloudless sky.

Rape me.

Creeping flesh, drips through my brain, handicaps me to
the brewing storm and the raindrops falling around while
the sky crashes down on me. From air bubbles, gurgle
arises the last breathe of sound the lips create. The simple
fragile skull burst and splits open oozes the precious liquid
of life. The ruins of the belly and the heavy intestine run
down the thigh and spits out the last golden dream.

A heavy shroud lays over the city. A murk, too thick to swim through, imprisons the once hovering angel under a cloudless sky. The body now burns passionate secret heat and desires like perfume above a sea of women. It embodied the mind with the allure of black decaying thoughts of gapping hollow wounds in loins.

The soul of the room bathes in idleness with a scent of regret and desire. The furniture languidly tossed is endowed with sleepwalking life. It cradles the drowsy spirit in a silent language. The unanalyzed impression of a broken heart and shattered will keeps the walls bare with the subtle clarity and hard to swallow obscurity of harmony. While staring through the window, it is a hellish dream I'm in that I wish no one to breathe in the sourness of its desolation.

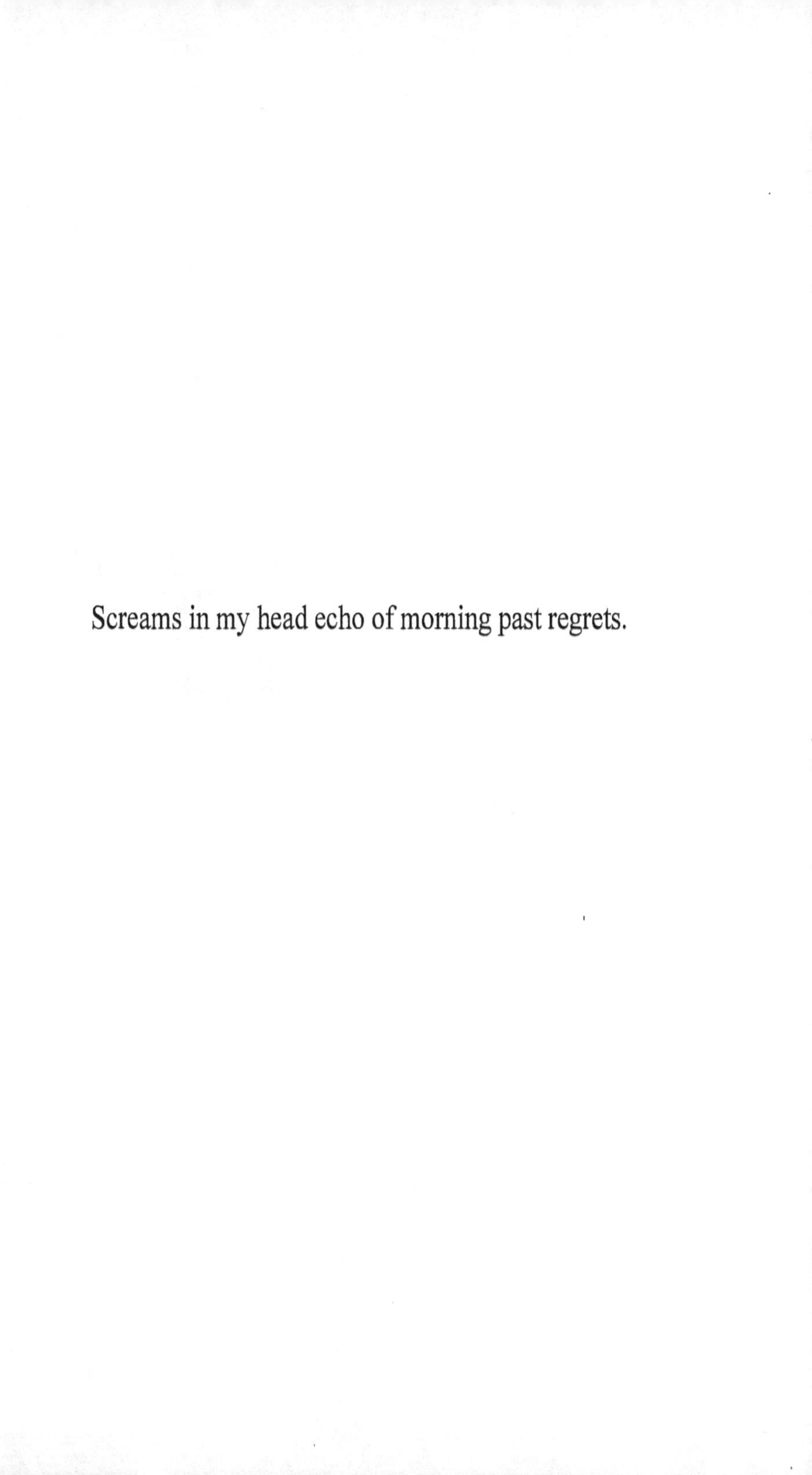

Screams in my head echo of morning past regrets.

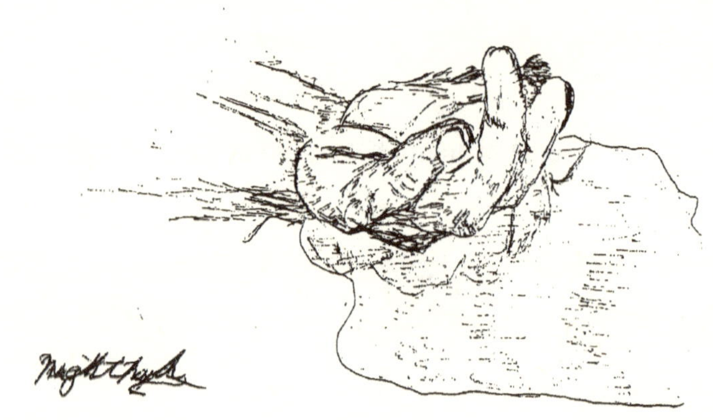

I cannot go on…

Libido steams infecting whore. Games of passion taste so sweet. Cut her throat slaughter the meat. Darkened voices bleed disease – dismembering me.

With insanity's dream hidden in the shroud of the cloud, people hurt. Shrieking ghostly howls, people cry in this bizarre livid sky; tormented by the thoughts descending deep in the shallow soul. Insatiability draws to the obscure and uncertain like voices that painfully inflict. The noises keep you insane. Skies tear over the house of the alive where mourning black clouds lay in wait. There is darkness and silence inside where water drips off the roof of the skull, the hearse of dreams. There is nothing there outside but the faint echo of silence in the dark daylight of a long drawn out funeral procession. Hope wean defeated, the phone never rings. The ears spawned have been cruelly forced deaf to the quiet noise.

Hate

Bloodletting

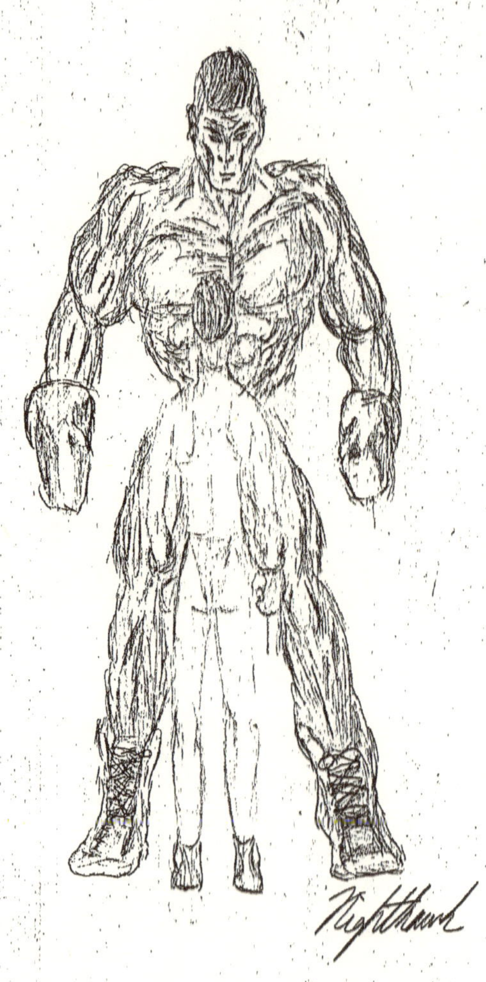

Rage

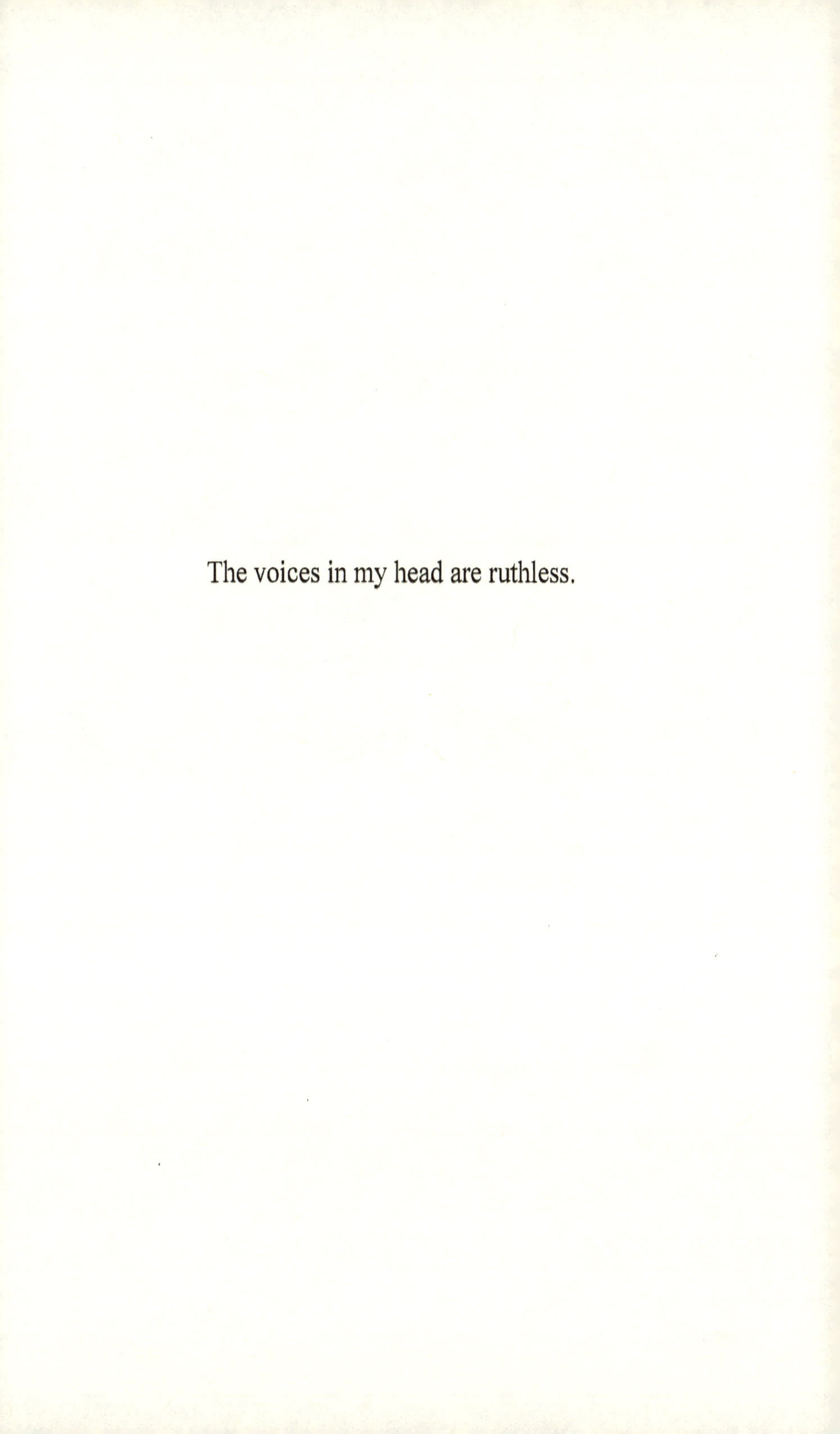

The voices in my head are ruthless.

I am at one with the silence. I found peace in the violence.

A dangling corpse, in a cold October night, keeps a hollow
eye on the eternal bed of winter snow dripping through and
time seeping past old frozen skeletons, hidden in the
closets, fretted by worms in the black dream that was
gusted open by melancholy from the past.

Pain

Alone

Failure

dreams fade, passion dies

Someone please save me as I drown.

Violent Pleasures

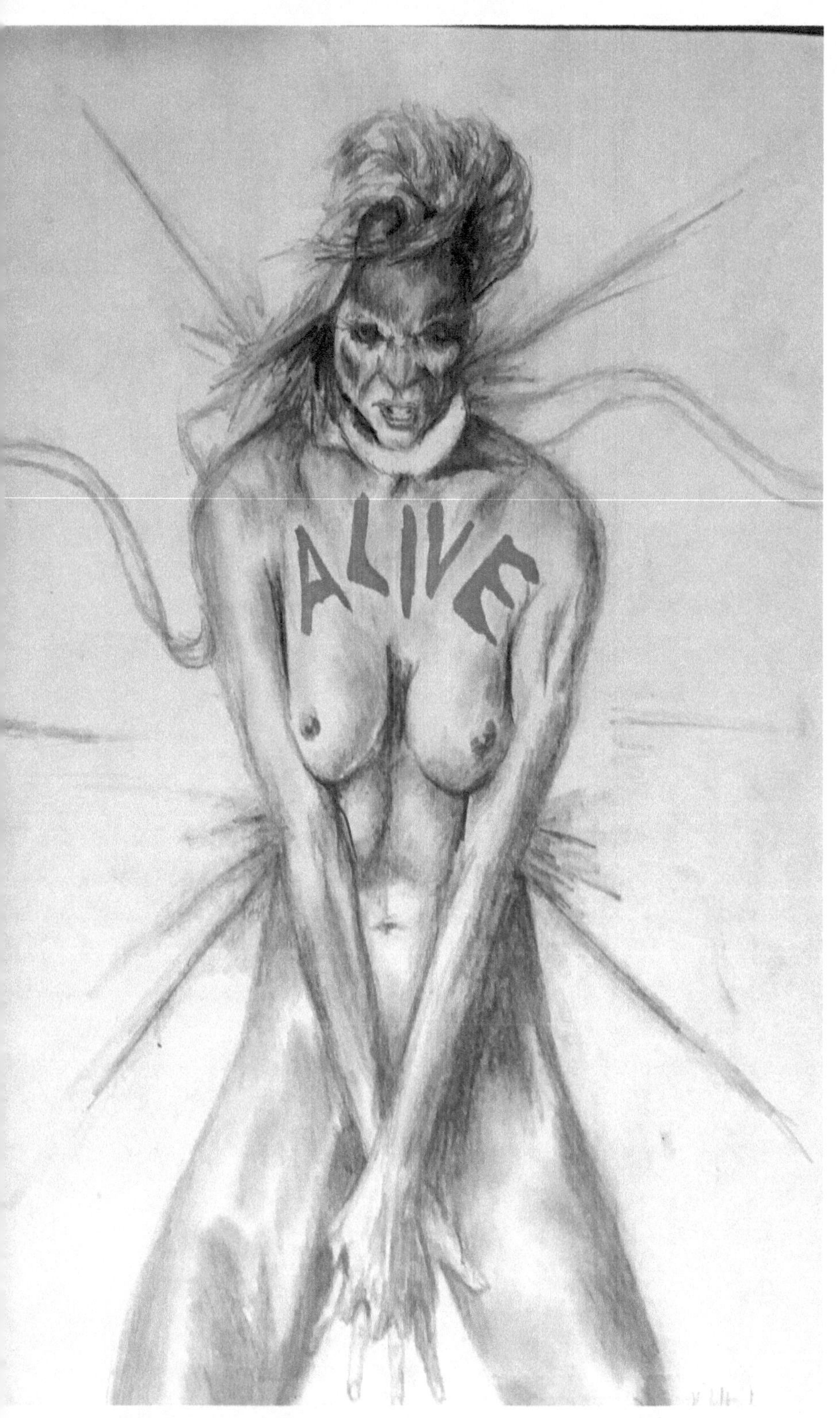
ALIVE

DEATH
OF
MOTHER
TECHNOLOGY

Suck me dry.

THE END

www.ingramcontent.com/pod-product-compliance
Lightning Source LLC
Chambersburg PA
CBHW031317130726

47988CB00007B/2867